BUGS, SPIDERS AND INSECTS!

A FUN ACTIVITY BOOK FOR ALL AGES

D1716346

Hello!

Welcome to this super amazing book and thank you for purchasing (or, if it's a gift and you're the recipient — thanks for reading!). You'll also soon be sketching, searching and solving, because this book is virtually brimming with fun activities to complete, all with a creepy-crawly theme (unless you count butterflies — which we do!).

So grab yourself;

A ballpoint

A pencil

A rubber

A ruler

A pair of eyes (preferably your own)

...and let's begin!

ANSWERS TO PUZZLES CAN BE FOUND AT THE END OF THE BOOK!

YOUR NAME

YOUR NAME IF YOU WERE A BUTTERFLY

YOU'RE NOT A TRIPLET!

TWO SETS OF BUTTERFLIES AREN'T TRIPLETS. CAN YOU SPOT WHICH?

BUTTERFLY SPOTTING WHICH IS THE RAREST?

CLONE THE INSECT!

See if you can give the insects an identical twin!

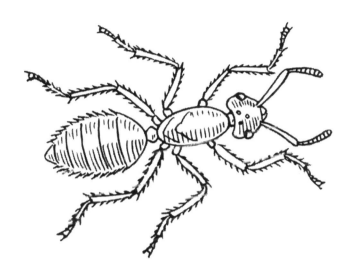

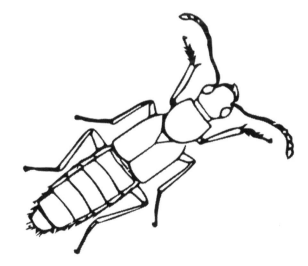

GRASSHOPPERS VS BEETLES

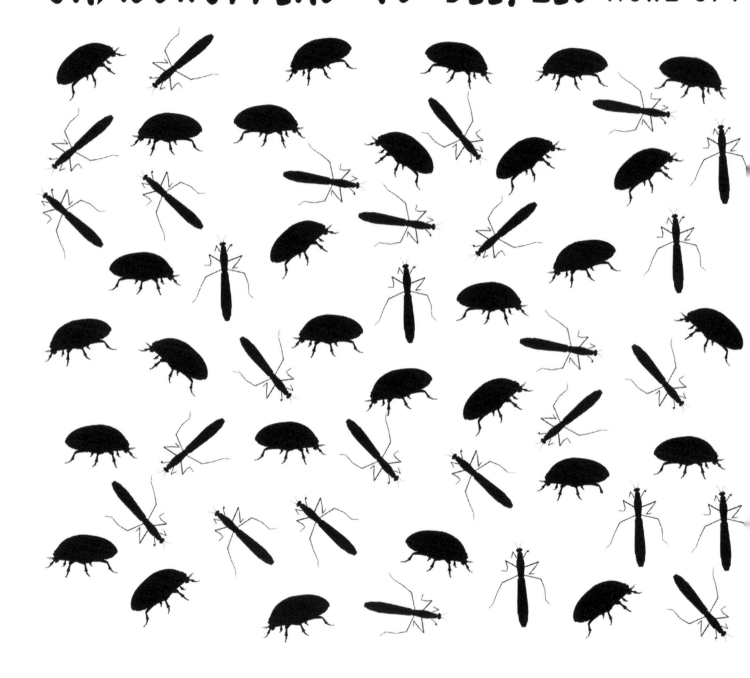

Grab your colouring pencils!

INSECTS AND BUGSEARCH!

T	P	O	L	E	E	L	A	S	O	A	T	O	E
M	S	O	E	T	O	T	E	E	S	S	M	T	I
C	O	M	P	U	U	G	I	P	P	E	E	I	S
B	T	O	S	S	O	R	W	M	S	R	E	U	S
U	E	E	C	R	W	A	S	P	R	E	O	Q	I
P	L	E	R	T	S	S	A	A	T	E	W	S	T
R	I	E	T	L	A	S	F	I	E	E	T	O	N
M	A	Y	F	L	Y	H	G	I	G	L	R	M	A
L	A	A	S	U	E	O	B	S	C	A	F	I	M
Y	E	P	A	O	O	P	T	E	K	C	I	R	C
E	A	R	W	I	G	P	E	S	C	L	E	U	B
M	I	A	T	U	A	E	E	O	T	E	T	L	I
N	O	K	E	E	H	R	L	R	S	A	G	I	T
I	T	E	R	S	E	P	E	E	I	E	O	E	E

MAYFLY
FLEA
MANTIS
GRASSHOPPER
WASP
LOUSE
CRICKET
BEETLE
MOSQUITO
TERMITE
EARWIG

TWO RARE!

WHERE'S THE BUG?

U B G G G B B U B G U G B B
U G B U B G B G U G B U U G
B U U G G G U G B G B U B G
B U B G U G U G G B U U B G
U B B U B G B G B G B G B U
U G U G U G G B U B G U G G
B U B U U B B U B U U G U G

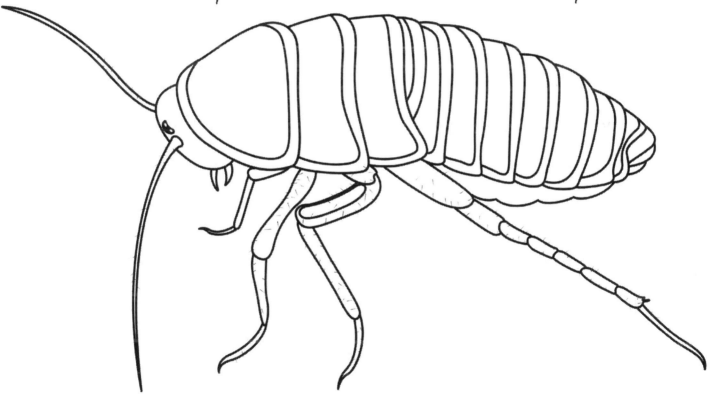

COLOUR THE COCKROACH!

Can you make him pretty?

THROUGH THE HIVE!

HELP BUZZER GET TO THE OTHER SIDE!

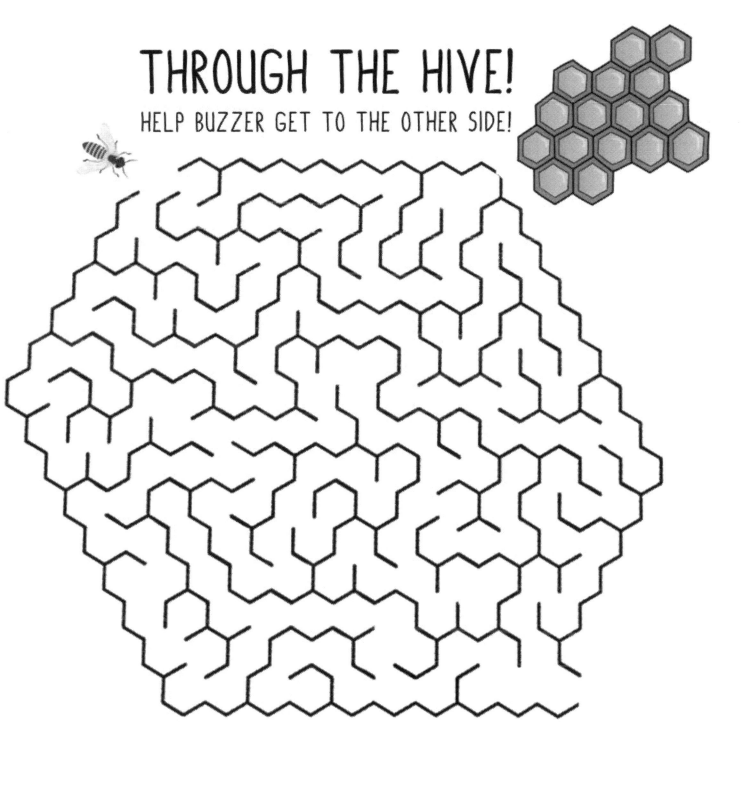

WHAT'S THE SPIDER?

D _ _ D _ L _ _ _ L _ _ S

GO _ _ E O _ B - WE _ _ ER

H _ _ T _ _ AN

_ A _ S _ W _ D _ W

H _ _ V _ _ TM _ _

_ _ ACK _ A _ E - _ E _ _ ER

LO _ E _ A G _ _ P _

SPOT THE TWO PAIRS!

COUNT THE BUGS!

WATCH OUT FOR THE PESKY EIGHT-LEGGED SPIDERS (THEY AREN'T BUGS!)

DESIGN YOUR OWN BUG OR INSECT INSPIRED JUMPER!

SPIDERS VS WEBS WHICH IS THERE MORE OF?

WHERE'S MY TWIN?
which route should he take?

A

B

C

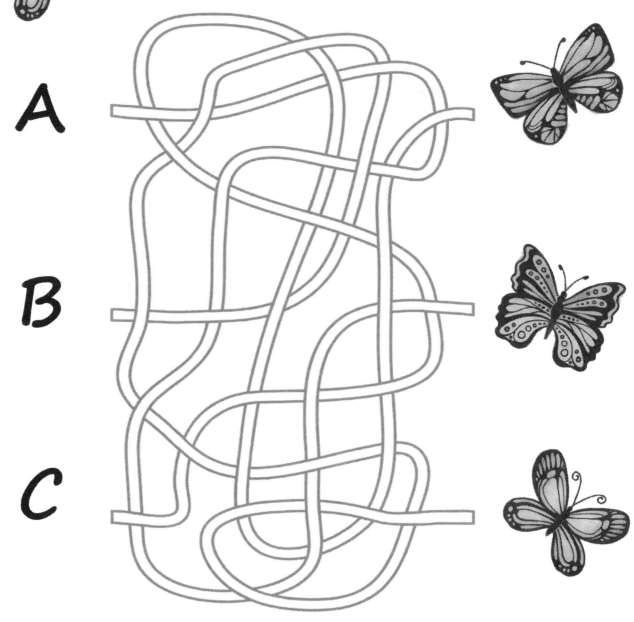

CLONE THE BUTTERFLIES!

See if you can give the butterflies an identical twin!

WAITER, THERE'S A FLY IN MY SOUP! HOW MANY SOUPS ARE FLY-FREE?

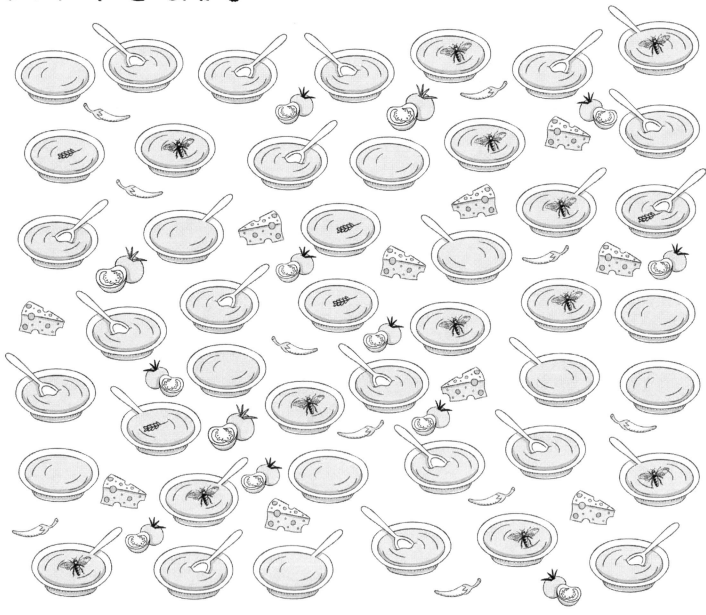

Colour in time!

BEEMOJIS! Who's the rarest?

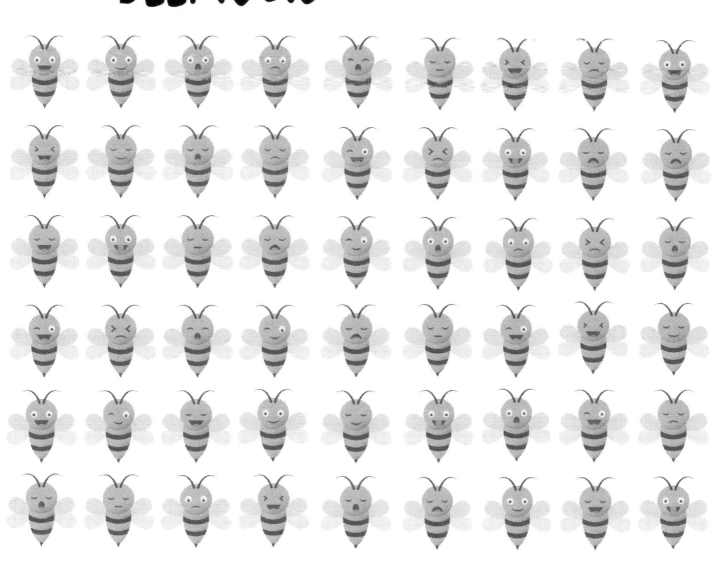

ANNIE AIN'T OK!

HELP ANNIE ANT ESCAPE THE MAZE

SAVE THE SPIDER!

DRAW SOMETHING
TO STOP SPIDEY
FALLING INTO THE
POT. BE CREATIVE!

SPOT THE TWO PAIRS!

GRAB YOUR
COLOURING
PENCILS!

YOU'RE NOT A TRIPLET!

THREE BUTTERFLIES AREN'T TRIPLETS. CAN YOU SPOT WHICH?

COUNT THE LOVELY BUTTERFLIES!

TOTAL

=

THE ROAD TO HONEY!

HELP THE BEE BACK TO THE NEST!

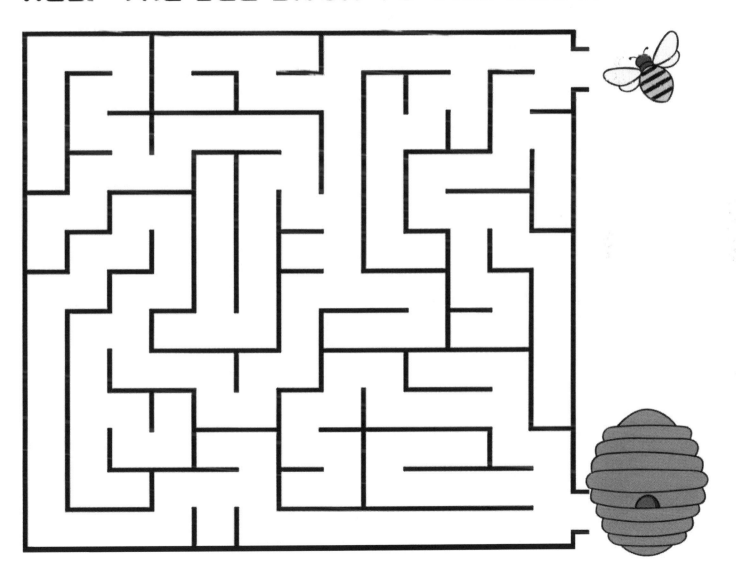

MY BIG BUG, SPIDER AND INSECT LIST!

List all the insects, spiders and bugs you can think of (you can come back to this when you find/think of another one!) See if you can fill up the page!

Colour me in!

WHERE'S THE ANT?

```
N A T T T A A N A T A T N T A A
N T A N A T A T A T N T A N N T
A N N T N T N T A T A T A N A T
A N A T N T N T T A N N A T
N A A N A T A T A T A T A T N N
N T N T N T T A N A T N A T
A N A N N A A N A N A N N T N T
```

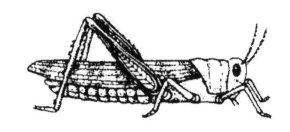

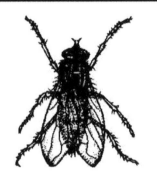

WHAT AM I?

HOUSEFLY   MOSQUITO
ANT   WASP
LADYBIRD   BUTTERFLY
LOCUST   BEE

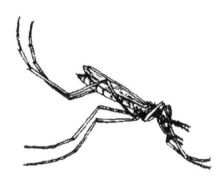

MISSING LEGS AND COBWEBS!

THERE ARE TWO SPIDERS MISSING A LEG AND TWO COBWEBS MISSING A STRAND. CAN YOU SPOT THEM?

SPIDER SEARCH!

H	U	N	T	S	M	A	N	L	R	R	C	A	S
A	E	R	A	G	E	L	E	N	I	D	A	E	S
D	S	S	M	B	L	A	C	K	W	I	D	O	W
D	E	A	U	I	P	O	R	D	W	E	D	N	C
T	I	E	L	L	S	A	S	E	A	L	N	P	E
A	E	E	E	R	C	S	T	L	R	L	C	A	L
S	X	G	A	A	C	E	U	I	L	L	A	R	E
A	K	N	E	L	E	T	R	L	H	A	E	S	R
D	N	E	T	N	N	S	K	S	E	E	O	O	C
A	A	T	I	A	A	A	D	R	A	N	R	N	R
D	X	E	R	G	E	R	D	G	D	X	A	A	A
N	E	A	T	R	B	A	I	P	C	E	R	B
G	T	A	L	R	G	C	S	A	O	R	A	T	R
L	T	E	M	R	N	K	O	S	E	N	S	N	T

BLACK WIDOW
TARANTULA
HUNTSMAN
TEGENARIA
AGELENIDAE
MISSULENA
TEXAS RECLUSE
CELER CRAB
DEWDROP
PARSON

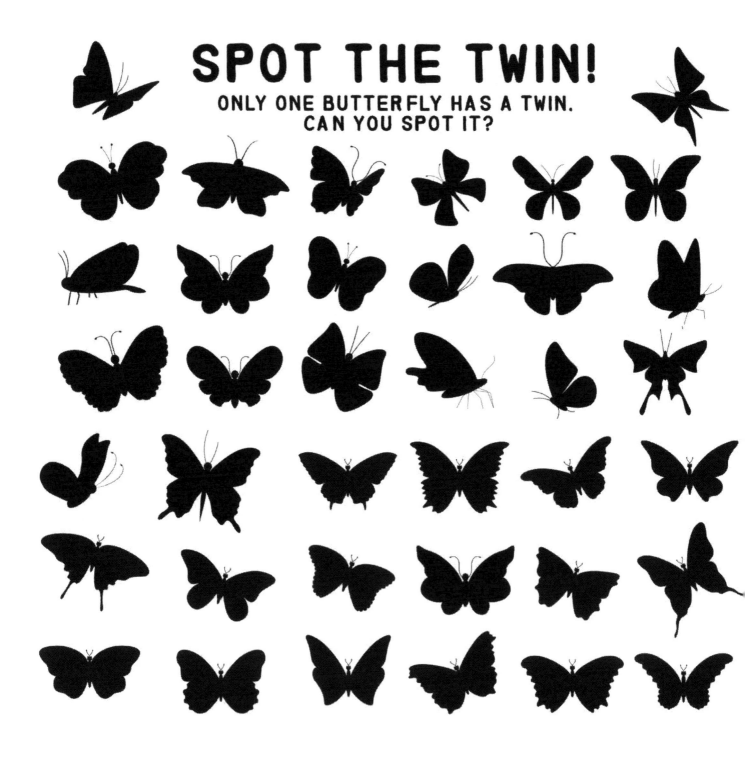

SPOT THE TWIN!

ONLY ONE BUTTERFLY HAS A TWIN.
CAN YOU SPOT IT?

CLONE THE INSECT!

See if you can give the insects an identical twin!

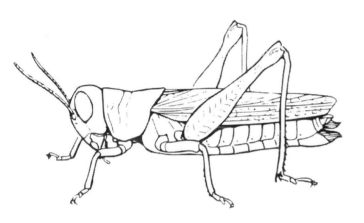

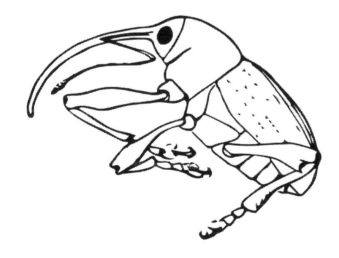

Colour me in!

MANTIS VS FLY

which is there more of?

WHICH WAY TO THE WEB?

HELP THE SPIDER BACK UP TO THE WEB!

COUNT the BEETLES!

GRAB YOUR
COLOURING
PENCILS!

Sketch Time!

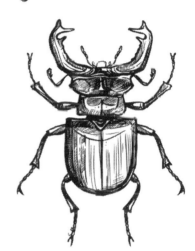

WHAT'S THE INSECT?

M _ _ L _ O _ M

D _ R _ L _ _ G B _ _ T _ E

DA _ _ EL _ L _

_ _ LE _ _ IC _ _ T

EM _ _ R _ R G _ M MO _ _

CI _ A _ A _

W _ _ _ E _ _ Y

COLOUR
THE PRETTY
BUGS!

WHICH INSECT GETS TO MEET ITS TWIN?

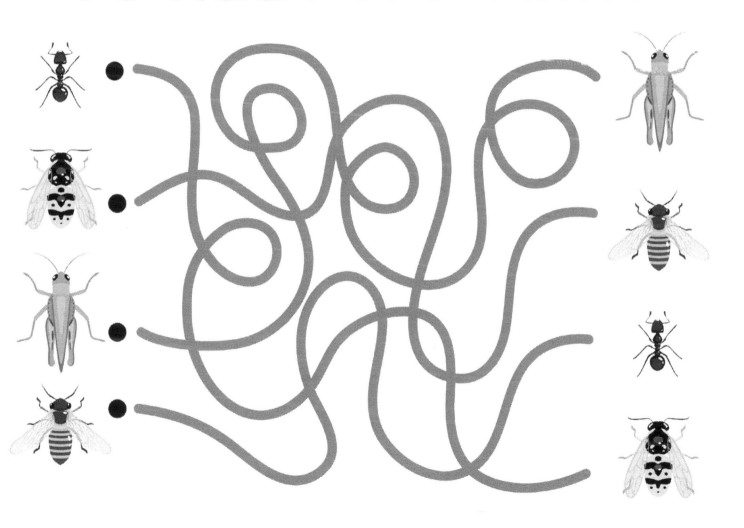

CLONE THE BUTTERFLIES!

See if you can give the butterflies an identical twin!

ANSWERS

WHAT'S THE SPIDER?

DADDY LONGLEGS
GORSE ORB-WEAVER
HUNTSMAN
FALSE WIDOW
HARVESTMAN
BLACK LACE-WEAVER
LOBED ARGIOPE

WHICH WAY TO THE WEB?
= B

WHERE'S MY TWIN: ROUTE TO TAKE
= B

WHICH INSECT GETS TO MEET ITS TWIN?
= GRASSHOPPER

COUNT THE LOVELY BUTTERFLIES
TOTAL = 25

COUNT THE BEETLES - 57

WHAT'S THE INSECT?

MEALWORM
DARKLING BEETLE
DAMSELFLY
MOLE CRICKET
EMPEROR GUM MOTH
CICADAS
WHITEFLY

SPOT THE TWO PAIRS!

YOU'RE NOT A TRIPLET!

TWO SETS OF BUTTERFLIES AREN'T TRIPLETS. CAN YOU SPOT WHICH?

MISSING LEGS AND COBWEBS!

THERE ARE TWO SPIDERS MISSING A LEG AND TWO COBWEBS MISSING A STRAND. CAN YOU SPOT THEM?

BUTTERFLY SPOTTING WHICH IS THE RAREST?

YOU'RE NOT A TRIPLET!

BUTTERFLIES AREN'T TRIPLETS. CAN YOU SPOT WHICH?

SPOT THE TWIN!

ONLY ONE BUTTERFLY HAS A TWIN.
CAN YOU SPOT IT?

TWO RARE!

THERE ARE 2 UNIQUE
BUTTERFLIES BELOW.
CAN YOU SPOT
THEM?

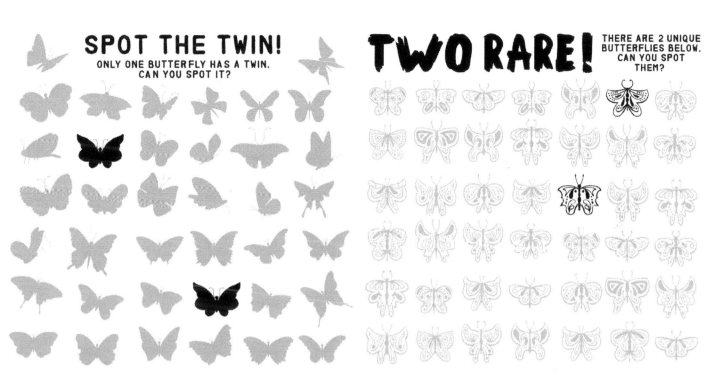

THE RARE BUTTERFLY

Can you spot the one unique butterfly?

BEEMOJIS! who's the rarest?

THE ROAD TO HONEY!
HELP THE BEE BACK TO THE NEST!

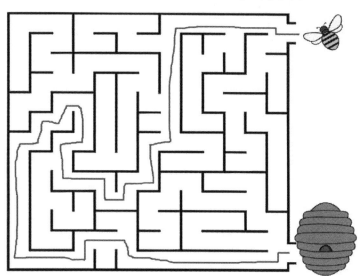

THROUGH THE HIVE!
HELP BUZZER GET TO THE OTHER SIDE!

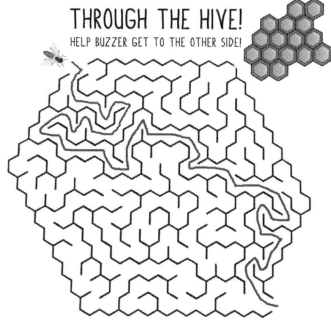

ANNIE AIN'T OK!

HELP ANNIE ANT
ESCAPE THE MAZE

LADYBIRD

LOCUST

BUTTERFLY

HOUSEFLY

WHAT AM I?

WASP

ANT

BEE

MOSQUITO

INSECTS AND BUGSEARCH!

T	P	O	L	E	E	E	L	A	S	O	A	T	O	E
M	S	O	E	T	O	T	E	E	S	S	M	T	I
C	O	M	P	U	U	G	I	P	P	E	E	I	S
B	T	O	S	S	O	R	W	M	S	R	E	U	S
U	E	E	C	R	W	A	S	P	R	E	O	Q	I
P	L	E	R	T	S	S	A	A	T	E	W	S	T	N
R	I	E	T	L	A	S	F	I	E	E	T	O	N
M	A	Y	F	L	Y	H	G	I	G	L	R	M	A
L	A	A	S	U	E	O	B	S	C	A	F	I	M
Y	E	P	A	O	O	P	T	E	K	C	I	R	C
E	A	R	W	I	G	P	E	S	C	L	E	U	B
M	I	A	T	U	A	E	E	O	T	E	T	L	I
N	O	K	E	E	H	R	L	R	S	A	G	I	T
I	T	E	R	S	E	P	E	E	I	E	O	E	E

SPIDERSEARCH!

H	U	N	T	S	M	A	N	L	R	R	C	A	S
A	E	R	A	G	E	L	E	N	I	D	A	E	S
D	S	S	M	B	L	A	C	K	W	I	D	O	W
D	E	A	U	I	P	O	R	D	W	E	D	N	C
T	I	E	L	L	S	A	S	E	A	L	N	P	E
A	E	E	E	R	C	S	I	L	R	L	C	A	L
S	X	G	A	A	C	E	I	L	L	A	R	E
A	K	N	E	L	C	T	R	L	H	A	E	S	R
D	N	E	T	N	N	S	K	S	E	E	O	O	C
A	A	T	I	A	A	A	D	R	A	N	R	N	R
D	X	E	R	G	E	R	D	G	D	X	A	A	A
N	E	A	T	R	B	A	I	A	P	C	E	R	B
G	T	A	L	R	G	C	S	A	O	R	A	T	R
L	T	E	M	R	N	K	O	S	E	N	S	N	T

WHERE'S THE ANT?

N	A	T	T	T	A	A	N	A	T	N	T	A	A
N	T	A	N	A	T	A	T	N	T	A	N	N	T
A	N	N	T	N	T	N	T	A	T	A	N	A	T
A	N	A	T	N	T	N	T	T	A	N	N	A	T
N	A	A	N	A	T	A	T	A	T	A	T	N	N
N	T	N	T	N	T	T	A	N	A	**T**	**N**	**A**
A	N	A	N	N	A	A	N	A	N	N	T	N	T

WHERE'S THE BUG?

U	B	G	G	G	B	B	U	B	G	U	G	B	B
U	G	B	U	B	G	B	G	U	G	B	U	U	G
B	U	U	G	G	G	U	G	B	G	B	U	B	G
B	U	B	G	U	G	U	G	G	B	U	U	B	G
U	B	B	U	B	G	B	G	B	G	B	G	B	U
U	G	U	G	U	G	G	B	U	B	G	U	G	G
B	U	B	U	U	B	B	U	B	U	U	G	U	G

SPIDERS VS COBWEBS
ANSWER- THERE ARE MORE SPIDERS
(32 SPIDERS, 31 COBWEBS)

GRASSHOPPERS VS BEETLES
ANSWER = THERE ARE MORE BEETLES
(29 BEETLES, 28 GRASSHOPPERS)

MANTIS VS FLY
ANSWER = THERE ARE MORE FLIES
(28 FLIES, 27 MANTIS)

COUNT THE BUGS
ANSWER = 43

HOW MANY ANTS IN
THE CIRCLE?   71

WAITER, THERE IS A
FLY IN MY SOUP - 32

THE LOST
LADYBIRD

SPOT THE TWO PAIRS!

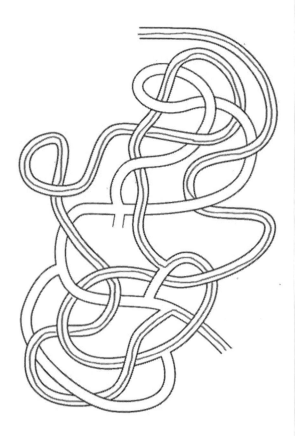

OTHER ACTIVITY BOOKS ALSO AVAILABLE!

CATS, KITTENS AND CATS!

DOGS, PUPPIES AND DOGS!

BIRDS, OWLS AND BIRDS!

FISH, DOLPHINS AND FISH!

ANIMALS IN THE WILD!

ANIMALS ON THE FARM!

HAPPY HALLOWEEN!

MERRY CHRISTMAS!

SUPERHEROES!

MONSTERS!

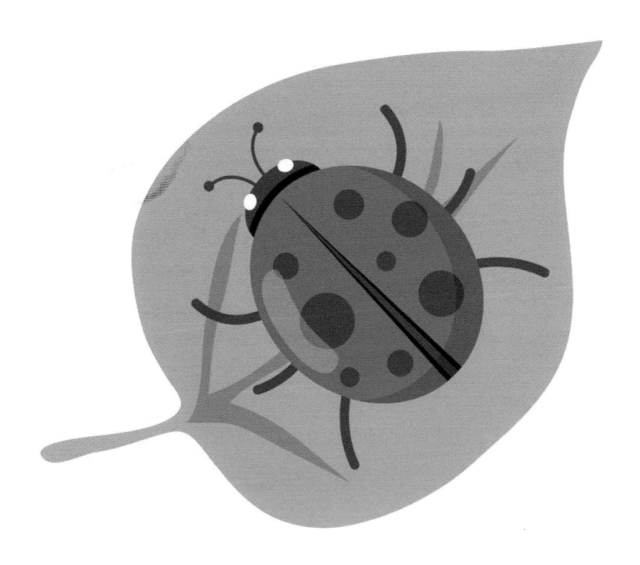

Images and vectors by;

freepix, alekksall, art.shcherbyna, agnessz_arts, anggar3ind, Alliesinteractive, Anindyanfitri, Ajipebriana, Alliesinteractive, Balasoui, Bakar015, Bimbimkha, brgfx, cornecoba, creativepack, creativetoons, ddraw, dooder, drawnhy97, elsystudio, Emily_b, flaticon, freshgraphix, frimufilms, Garrykillian, gordoba, graphicrepublic, iconicbestiary, Jannoon028, johndory, Kamimiart, kat_branch, kbibibi, Kjpargeter, layerace, lesyaskripak, lexamer, lyolya_profitrolya, Macrovector, Makyzz, milano83, nenilkime, natalka_dmitrova, natkacheva, omegapics, Pickapic, rawpixel, Rayzong, renata.s, rezzaalam, rocketpixel, RosaPuchalt, Rwdd_studios, sketchepedia, stephanie2212, SilviaNatalia, Terdpongvector, titusurya, vectorpocket, Vectortwins, Vector4free, vectorportal, vectorpouch, vecteezy, VVstudio, Visnezh, zirconicusso

60169894R00041

Made in the USA
Columbia, SC
12 June 2019